CW00410499

Disclai...

The information given in thi...
my opinion, my understandi..., ... p... ...
the rules in force and my knowledge.

It is not authoritative and cannot be considered as such.

Despite all the precautions and verifications made, no responsibility for inaccuracy, error or omission can be held. Similarly, it cannot be held responsible for any damage resulting directly or indirectly from the information in this book.

Thus, each person wishing to intervene in his or her car should consult his or her own advisors and professionals in order to appreciate the information contained in this book.

Introduction

Preparing your car is not trivial, you must not forget to take into account the regulatory side, as well as the purely mechanical aspect.

This book is not intended to influence the preparation but simply to understand and inform about good practices. If you choose to enter this process, you must do so with full knowledge of the causes. It is therefore a simple presentation of the existing with the basics of operation as well as my advice and tips.

Some solutions are valid for one vehicle but not for all. Before taking the plunge, make sure you are well informed about your car.

Passionate about mechanics, after a DUT in mechanical engineering, followed by an engineering school, I became a racing engineer in motor sports, with a diploma of "preparer and developer of competition vehicles".

This course allowed me to acquire the basics in vehicle preparation.

That's why I observe many people, wanting to modify and customize their car, without having the knowledge. My objective is to present to you the functioning of the different parts, to enlighten the choices of some, and to help the individuals and amateurs in their projects. These modifications must preserve the safety of the users (internal and external to the vehicle) as well as the mechanics.

I will therefore try to enlighten you and show you what can be done, without going into too many technical considerations.

It is rather intended for recent vehicles, with electronic management. It allows amateurs to lay the foundations, to propose ideas for:

- Improve performance

- Add and/or modify equipment

- Customize

Namely, it is easier and less expensive to obtain gains on a turbo engine than on an atmospheric (=without turbo) The increase in power will therefore be more complicated on older cars (carburetor and/or atmospheric engines).

However, whatever your vehicle, including diesel vehicles, the adjustment of the chassis part will always be valid.

Contents

• Disclaimer   P1

• Introduction   P2

• Author   P3

• The Book   P4

• The Law – Legal Aspect   P6

• Definitions   P7

• Engine or Chassis ?   P8

• Frame   P9 – P37

• Engine   P38 – P61

• Body and Interior   P62 – P68

• Electronics   P69 – P74

• Conclusion   P75 – P77

• Appendix   P78

Legislation – The Law

However, the law is still rather vague about whether it is allowed to drive modified cars. The police tolerate certain transformations, and the only thing that is mandatory is that your vehicle passes the technical inspection. The law requires insurance! And in your insurance contract the car must be in conformity with the manufacturer's data (its factory specifications). That's why any modification is forbidden, without having passed the legal authorities authorizations, which is the homologation body. This process is long and costly, so most people don't go through with it or don't take the risk.

In case of an accident, if you have modified your vehicle, there is a risk of not being followed by your insurance.

For each modification, you must check what the law says, to know what the limits are not to exceed.

Definitions

Motor: It is a device allowing a transformation of any energy into a mechanical energy.

In our case, it is an internal combustion engine, which is under your hood. It transforms thermal energy from combustion into mechanical energy for rotation.

Frame: It is the rigid structure and the basic structure of your car. It is on this base that all the parts come to be grafted.

In everyday language, we often call the chassis, which corresponds, in fact, to the links to the ground and thus to the mechanical parts causing the behavior of your car.

Understeer: It corresponds to the loss of grip of the front wheels. In a curve, the car seems to want to go straight.

On a curve: This corresponds to the loss of grip of the rear wheels. This is the case when you spin or drift, the car "survives".

Engine or Frame ?

The chassis is the most important! It is the base and structure of the vehicle.

You can have an engine as big and as powerful as you want if the chassis doesn't follow, you won't get any gain. Except if you want to do exclusively RUN (straight line racing only), for which the engine preparation will be essential. But for daily use and/or on track, the importance should be focused on the behavior and the driving.

In addition to being the link between you and the road, the chassis can be considered as a safety element, as it includes the ground connections (wheels).

So, to understand the whole reaction of the car and its chassis, it is necessary to understand the dynamics of the vehicle. This subject will be partially discussed in this book.

FRAME

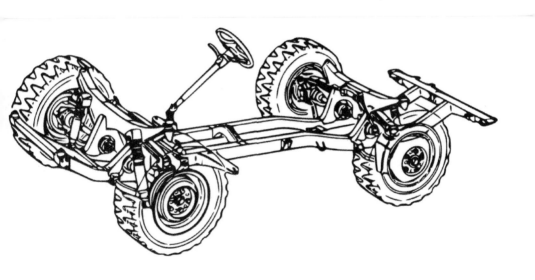

Frame – Definition

Ground connections: Corresponds to all the elements that make the connection between the ground and your chassis. These elements are generally linked together and we find:

- Axle

- Wheels

- Direction

- Suspension

- Brakes

Geometry: Making a geometry corresponds to making an adjustment of body height, parallelism, camber and caster. On most production cars, only the front wheel alignment is adjustable without modifications.

A wheel is a tire + rim assembly.

tire

rim

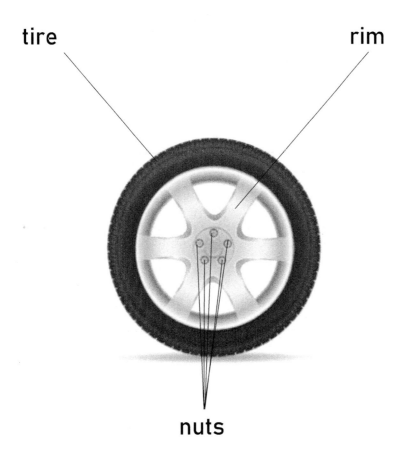

nuts

11

Frame - Tires

Tires are the most important element ! They are the link between your car and the ground.

A chassis preparation, as consequent and expensive as it is, is useless if the tires are not in good condition and of good quality. They are the first elements of safety, have a direct influence on the road holding and it is therefore essential to regularly check them (wear, pressure).

Therefore, you should consider your tires in your budget and go for recognized brands for which reliability, efficiency and endurance are no longer to be proven.

Structure : AAA/BB/RCC DD E

- AAA: tire width in mm

- BB: sidewall height in % of the tire width

- R: tire structure (radial, diagonal or cross belt)

- CC: Inside diameter in inches

- DD: Load index (appendix)

- E: Speed index (appendix)

There are other indications on the sidewall of a tire, such as its date of manufacture, the model, an arrow for the direction of rotation if it has one...

Exemple : 205/55/R16 91V

205: tire width in mm

55: sidewall height in % compared to the width of the tire:

205 x 55% = mm112,75

R: Radial tire

16: inside diameter in inches

91: Load index (appendix) = Kg615

V: Speed index (appendix) = km/h240

Manufacturers offer different ranges:

- **Budget**: Entry level, to get equipped at a lower cost. Hard tires, with a random road holding according to the chosen brand

- **Quality**: High quality tires with the best quality/price ratio

- **Premium**: Made by the big brands, they are more expensive but the handling is much better

- **Sport**: They are soft, have a shorter lifespan, are quite expensive, but the road holding is excellent and allow to satisfy the amateurs of strong sensations

If you have the opportunity to put Slicks tires (forbidden on public roads) on your production car, **I advise you against it!** Tires can take so much stress that I've already seen some chassis bend. If you still want to try it, reinforce your frame and put anti- twist bars.

Frame – Choice of tires

We also find tires:

- **Winter**: Its composition and structure are developed and worked to provide a good grip on wet, icy or snowy roads. These tires are more efficient than summer tires when the temperature drops below the freezing point.7

- **Mixed or 4-season**: These tires offer a good alternative for those who do not wish to change tires all year round. These tires offer good handling on wet roads and are less noisy than winter tires. However, their handling on snow is not as good as a winter tire, and not as good as a summer tire in hot weather.

The best solution is to have 8 complete balanced wheels, with four summer tires, and with four winter tires.

Frame – Rims

They are the link between your tires and your chassis. Changing your rims therefore implies respecting:

- Nut spacing (distance between nut holes)

- Rim diameter (in inches)

- Rim width

- Offset (ET)

- Central Bore

1) Taking rims with different nut centers is simply impossible and you will not be able to mount them on your vehicle without using shims.

2) It is possible to change the rim diameter, but you must consult a correspondence table or ask your technical control if there are tires that fit this new size. Indeed, by changing your rim diameter, if you do not find tires with the same wheel circumference as the original, your speedometer and odometer will be distorted.

3) Fitting wider rims can allow you to fit different sized tires or, for example, stretched blanks.

4) The offset is the distance between the rim attachment and the edge of the rim. It is noted in mm.

5) The center bore corresponds to the center diameter of the rim and therefore to the diameter of your hub. For aftermarket rims (= not original), it is possible to have spacers/shims to match.

- The weight is not negligible.

- The rim is an unsprung element, so it follows the undulations of the road. In comparison, an unsprung element of kg1, corresponds to several kg on a suspended element (example: an element in the passenger compartment).

- So, the more weight an unsprung mass has, the more force your engine will need to accelerate or brake it. Therefore, reducing the mass of one of these elements will allow for more powerful acceleration and braking, and therefore gain in performance.

You will easily understand that it is easier to stop a wheel of 1 kg than a wheel of 100 kg because it develops less inertia. That's why the weight of your wheels will have an influence on your performance during acceleration and braking, but also on your fuel consumption.

As the name suggests, track wideners increase the track of a vehicle. The track is the distance between the 2front or 2rear wheels. (The wheelbase is the distance between the axis of the front wheels and the rear wheels)

Increasing the track allows for better handling and cornering stability, as well as a better appearance of your car with a more powerful and sporty feel. On the other hand, track wideners influence the wear of your steering parts and wheel bearings.

There are single and double bolt wideners. As the name indicates, the simple bolts take the bolts of your wheel and are simply placed between the rim and the hub.

For small spacers, up to 5 mm, it is possible to use the original bolts, otherwise for larger spacers I advise to use extended nuts.

The double bolts are more adapted to big thicknesses and more secure. They consist of nuts to fix the spacer on the hub, then your original nuts to fix the wheel on the flare.

This modification corresponds to increasing the offset of your rim.

Double bolted wideners

Wheel chocks are an inexpensive and easy to do modification, with a low risk for your car (as long as you don't put too big chocks).

I don't recommend this system which for me is anti mechanical, we add weight on non-suspended masses, therefore additional rotating masses.

If you want to increase the track width of your vehicle, finding rims with a lower offset seems to me to be a much better solution. Your rims will stand out more, as well as improve your handling. If however, you can't buy new rims, small shims can be a good solution.

The suspension allows to make in part the road holding of your car, it ensures the contact between the wheels and the ground. It connects the suspended masses to the non-suspended masses. There are several types, and it is composed of several elements.

Shock absorber: Absorbs and dissipates the energy of shocks and road imperfections

Spring: It allows to press the wheel against the ground and to suspend the car

Spring

Shock absorber

Different suspension/shock absorber systems exist, I won't be able to present them all in this book: McPherson (the most used at the front on production cars), rigid axle, leaf springs, torsion bar, double wishbone (sports car),...

Everything can be changed independently:

- Putting sports shock absorbers will allow to have a better road handling, a firmer car with an increase of the hardness in compression as well as an often more dynamic rebound

- Changing the springs to short springs will lower the center of gravity of the car, thus reducing the roll of the car. However, you have to be careful not to lower the center of gravity too much, otherwise the shock absorbers will not work in the range of travel for which they were originally designed. It is also possible to change the material of the spring, or to have non-linear springs.

- Putting threaded handsets, seems the most complete choice, the most suitable but also the most expensive.

Frame – Suspension

The cheapest solution to improve the style of your car but also its handling seems to be short springs.

Many manufacturers offer them, with different discounts. If you want to mount them on original shocks, I can advise you not to take too low.

30 mm already seems not bad, beyond the wear of your shocks which will be really premature, the car may become uncomfortable.

These short springs are generally a little harder than the original ones. The resulting lowering will reduce the height of the car's center of gravity, thus increasing road holding, with less roll in curves.

For any change of suspension components, consider doing a vehicle geometry.

This is the suspension system found on racing/sport cars.

It is a shock absorber + spring assembly. It is possible to adjust the height of the spring, thus the height of the body. It can be adjusted according to your preferences and your use.

For example, it will be possible to lower the car to give a sporty character while it will be preferable to raise it for a 4X4 with the aim of making crossing.

On the other hand, the adjustments are mechanical, so the wheels must be removed to access them.

It is also common to be able to adjust the shock absorbers.

There are 2 types of adjustments, compression and rebound. They are done via a wheel: one for the compression and another for the rebound, or a wheel which combines the two. 2.

Before starting any modification adjustment, record your values, so you can easily go back if needed.

Preload: This is the amount of preload applied to the spring. First of all, unless you have a variable pitch spring, which is very rare, adjusting your preload will not make the assembly harder. It will simply raise or lower your vehicle.

Compression: Your shock absorber acts in compression when it compresses.

Relaxation: In a second time your shock absorber will return to its initial position, it is therefore in its relaxation phase. It is this phase that gives the feeling of comfort

For the higher end shocks, it is possible to adjust the compression and rebound on high and low speeds.

Camber: Looking at the car in its axis of travel. It is the angle formed by the vertical on the ground and the axis of the wheel passing through its center.

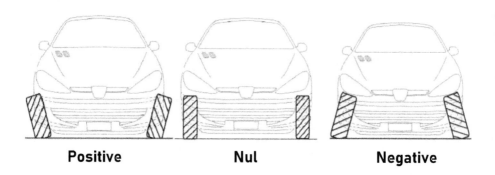

| Positive | Nul | Negative |

Adding negative camber allows you to gain grip in curves by compensating for the tire's deformation. It influences the contact area of the tire with the ground.

It is rare that the camber is adjustable on a production car. To adjust it in most cases you will need to mount threaded combinations with adjustable cups.

Adjusting the camber will affect the handling of your car, and the wear of your tires.

Parallelism: Looking at the car from above. It is the angle formed between the theoretical axis of travel of the wheel (parallel to the axis of the car) and the steering axis of the wheel.

Clamp   **Opening**

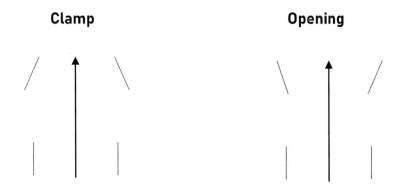

Modeling of the clamp and the opening on the front wheels, putting the clamp on the front will make the car sharper and more directive, while the opening will stabilize it by increasing understeer.

The opening at the rear will make the car oversteer, with a more playful rear end, while the clamp will promote stability.

The front parallelism is an easy adjustment to make, but in the rear, it is very rare that it is adjustable.

Caster: Looking at the car from the side. It is the angle formed between t h e vertical axis of the wheel and the axis of the pivot.

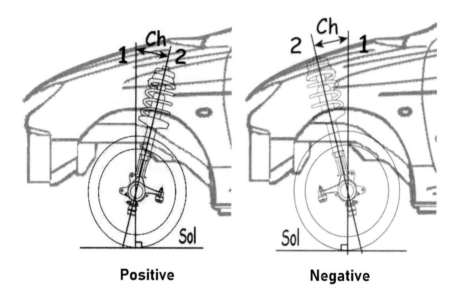

Positive   Negative

Increasing the caster angle stabilizes the car with speed, at the expense of handling.

You can significantly change the behavior of your car by changing your alignment setting.

Frame – Mount a roll bar

The roll bar is an essential element in motorsport, it is a safety element that protects the driver but also stiffens the structure of the vehicle and therefore improves its behavior.

There are bolt-on and weld-on ones.

If the roll bar is not original on your car, which is the case (unless you have a GT3 RS or other vehicle of this type), you must know :

• The parts are not approved,

• Safety: in the event of a collision, your car is supposed to deform, so if it doesn't deform or deforms only slightly, you risk causing more damage to the other vehicle and the occupants (from 2 cars). In case of a rollover, without a helmet, your head may hit the roll bar. Also, if an extrication is necessary, the roll bar may interfere with the work of the firefighters.

• Practicality: Depending on its shape and geometry, it can make it difficult to get in and out of your vehicle, both front and rear.

•

They can be mounted in front, behind, and even in the middle of the car. They are less dangerous than a roll bar and less expensive, therefore much more adapted to a sport use, allowing also to make some circuit outings.

These bars stiffen and reinforce the body, keeping the suspension geometry in place in order to absorb as much as possible the imperfections of the road.

At the front and rear, they must be mounted on the shock heads.

Frame – Bar anti-roll bar

The anti-roll bar or stabilizer bar or anti-roll bar is a suspension component that connects the two wheels of a single axle and limits body movements in curves.

Rolling is one of the movements that has proven to be uncomfortable. It is the rotation movement around the longitudinal axis of the car. When you see an old car (4L or 2CV) in a roundabout, it looks like it is going to roll over, or that its underbody is going to touch the ground, it is because it rolls. In comparison, today's cars roll much less, thanks to the anti-roll bars.

The modification of the anti-roll bars (by harder ones) is generally done only on the big preparations intended for the circuit. This results in a gain in performance, but also a change in the car's behavior (not necessarily a problem, on the contrary) and a loss of comfort. On the other hand, someone who wants to drive in the sand will have to remove them.

Frame – The Weight

Just as in sports, athletes seek to lose weight to improve their performance. It's the same for your car.

By decreasing its mass, your engine will have more ease, therefore increased performance, with increased agility.

Some people who want to race choose to empty their car.

Emptying your car is to prepare it as a race car by removing: the back seat, the carpets, the spare wheel, the soundproofing . . . Everything that is superfluous in racing!

Emptying the cabin makes the car lighter but can be a hassle on a daily basis.

You must be able to separate what you want to improve: endurance and/or power. Choose your evolutions according to what you want.

Since brakes are part of safety, you should not modify anything without mastering the subject or calling a professional. In addition, brake fluid deteriorates quickly as it heats up and loses its properties, so it is important to bleed/change it regularly.

Remember that this book is only an indication that modifying elements such as the braking is not harmless and therefore forbidden for a car running on open road. Moreover, each modification made involves your responsibility.

To improve the braking, several parts are subject to change:

- **Discs:** Sports discs, designed for performance, allow for better heat dissipation, reduce the risk of fogging, or vibrations.

- **Brake pads:** Like the discs, the sports pads, evacuate heat better and their friction coefficient is increased, to improve their behavior at high temperatures as well as endurance.

- **Brake Fluid:** As with racing cars, it is possible to use brake fluid with a higher boiling point, which will allow you to hold a higher brake pressure for a longer time.

- **Hoses:** Hoses expand (soft pedal feel) and become porous over time. To counter these phenomena there are aviation hoses, which are more resistant and therefore will improve your braking.

However, if these rather simple and inexpensive modifications don't work for you, you can always consider:

- Change your calipers: Put them with bigger pistons, or more pistons to increase the contact surface. Be careful with the passage in the rim.

- Increasing the diameter of the disc: This will result in a modification of the caliper support, but the heat dissipation will be greater and therefore the braking will be more durable.

- Adding cooling bails.

- Modify the master cylinder and its diameter (calculations are required), which will possibly modify the need to modify the pedal stroke.

- Change the distribution, by putting a splitter or changing the diameter of the hoses between the front and the rear.

ENGINE

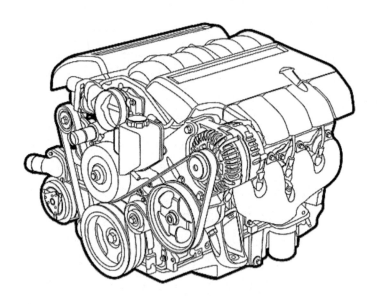

Your heat engine transforms energy, in our case combustion or explosion energy, into mechanical energy.

It works in 4 time,

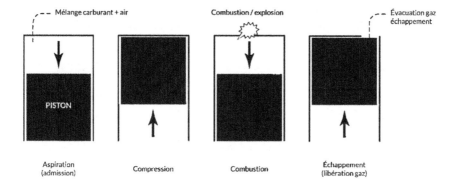

Mélange carburant + air   Combustion / explosion   Évacuation gaz échappement

PISTON

Aspiration (admission)   Compression   Combustion   Échappement (libération gaz)

The explosions push the pistons into a translational motion which is then transmitted to the crankshaft to become a rotational motion which is then transmitted via the gearbox to the wheels.

Several architectures exist:

• Online,

• In V,

• In W,

• In VR

The engine can be divided into 3 parts:

- The cylinder head (top of the engin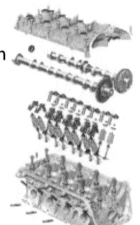

- Motor housing

- Lower engine (oil pan)

The oil has an essential role in its proper functioning and has a direct impact on performance. It allows:

- **Lubricate:** this is its main role, to ensure that all the mechanical parts move correctly in relation to each other.

- **Cooling:**Aqualityoilcontainspartoftheheatofyouren gine in addition to the coolant.

- **Cleaning:** it recovers the impurities, by through the oil filter.

- **Protect:** it prevents rusting and oxidation of your engine block.

All this justifies the use of a quality oil and regular oil changes. In addition to keeping your engine in shape, this will reduce fuel consumption, and an additive, antifriction, will smooth the engine behavior and limit the wear of internal parts even more.

Engine – Admission

The combustion occurs with a **mixture of air and fuel,** and the candle takes care of the explosion.

The air comes into the engine through the intake!

That's why a well-designed, high-performance intake is so important, because it will allow your engine to perform at its best.

Several types of intake exist, each with its own advantages depending on the type of engine.

On an atmospheric engine, the intake is at atmospheric pressure, unlike supercharged engines that are equipped with turbo or compression, on which the intake pressure is increased.

Original Air Filter: Often made of paper, it must be changed periodically. It works well and is inexpensive but is not optimized.

Sport Air Filter: Fitted in the original air box, allowing more air to pass than the manufacturer's filter. It can offer significant gains depending on the model, and cannot be changed, but can be cleaned and greased at regular intervals.

Direct Intake: The original air box is removed and the filter, which is often cone-shaped, is put on directly.

Dynamic Intake: We remove the original air box, and we add one, often in carbon, with an air intake in front, allowing to take much more fresh air.

For direct and dynamic intakes, on recent cars, be careful not to remove the air flow meter if you are equipped with it.

Gasoline engine: they create the spark allowing the air/fuel mixture to ignite, and thus the explosion, then the rotation.

They must be changed periodically, according to the manufacturer's recommendations, and even more frequently if your vehicle is prepared.

Be careful if you want to put more efficient spark plugs on some engines, it is better to put original ones and change them more frequently.

Diesel engine: they preheat the combustion chamber when starting, which is why they are called glow plugs and why you had to wait to start for a few seconds on older models.

Engine – Supercharging

Using an engine supercharger to increase its power aims to increase efficiency without increasing its speed.

It is difficult to increase the speed of a motor because you quickly reach the limit of the mechanical parts, which greatly affects reliability.

So, to increase the power, it is necessary to increase the torque, by increasing the quantity of the inflammable mixture, with a device of supercharging. The latter consists in injecting air under pressure to increase the power of the explosion. To pressurize the air a turbo or a compressor is used.

Turbocharger: This supercharging system is driven by the engine's exhaust gases. These gases drive a turbine, which compresses the gases via a second turbine, to finally send it into the engine under high pressure.

Compressor: This is driven by a belt, which is itself connected to the motor. It compresses the air and sends it under high pressure via two rotors.

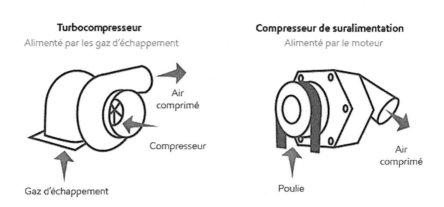

Turbocompresseur
Alimenté par les gaz d'échappement

Air comprimé

Compresseur

Gaz d'échappement

Compresseur de suralimentation
Alimenté par le moteur

Air comprimé

Poulie

Many modifications are possible depending on what you want to achieve and your budget: mounting a bigger turbo, modifying the existing one, lightening and changing the diameter of the compressor pulley …

Also known as a "relief valve", it is fitted to turbo engines and is mounted on the intake hose. It is an element that improves the reliability of the turbo and its reaction time, by avoiding a harmful phenomenon of counter pressure, wanting to make the turbo turn in the opposite direction.

In the case of an open circuit, it produces a distinct sound ("pschittt"), whereas in a closed circuit, the air is more quietly injected back into the intake manifold.

There are several technologies that should not be chosen at random. It is therefore necessary to find out what is most suitable for your vehicle.

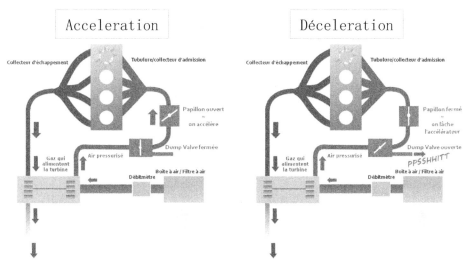

The WasteGate is also a valve, but it limits the pressure of the exhaust gases. It allows part of the exhaust gases to pass directly to the exhaust. Thus, by managing its opening, we can control the energy we want to recover from the turbine, the speed of rotation of the turbo and reduce the back pressure generated by the turbine at the exhaust.

It can be: mechanical, pneumatic, electrical or hydraulic.

Changing the opening and/or closing of the wastegate can change the power because it will affect the boost pressure.

Also known as the air/air exchanger, it is used on turbo engines and has a real influence on performance. It cools the gases before intake. The turbo compresses the gases to inject more, but this operation also heats them.

The hotter the air, the more it expands and the less dense it is. That's why, between the turbo and the intake, there is a heat exchanger, allowing them to cool.

Originally, the heat exchanger is often of average size, not always in front position on the car and does not allow to keep the engine power over long periods of high loads. Thus, in the aftermarket, we often find larger exchangers (higher cooling capacity) and positioned just in front of the grille to take a maximum of fresh air.

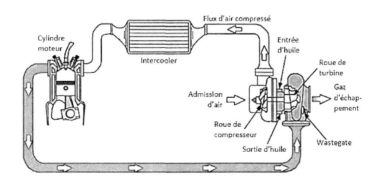

However, be careful not to mount an intercooler that is too big, compared to the turbo, because this will lead to an increase in the filling time (lag). This lag is felt by a delay in the response of the turbo, and therefore in the acceleration of your engine.

The exchanger must be adapted to the size of the parts present on the car and particularly the turbo to limit the loss of reactivity.

If by putting a bigger exchanger, the air is not cooled more than the original one, there is no interest, the quality of the exchanger body is thus essential.

Following the installation of the exchanger, reprogramming is mandatory to take advantage of the increase in power and to limit the lag.

The exhaust system is generally composed of a manifold, a catalytic converter, then mufflers2, an intermediate one (under the car) and a final muffler (at the back, the one you see).

It is quite common to remove one or both mufflers2 to increase the noise, this slightly increases the power since the gases are less retained.

Removing the catalytic converter will have the same effect, while being a little more important and bringing a gain of torque at low rpm. However, removing it will lead to excess pollution and will therefore be impossible to pass the technical inspection. Moreover, the vehicle will have to be reprogrammed to avoid engine defects.

Changing the manifold is also feasible, and there are manifolds in different shapes and materials. Find out what suits your engine and its reliability.

Engine – Exhaust system

We often hear about stainless steel exhaust systems. In addition to providing a strong and distinctive metallic sound, this material allows for an exhaust system that does not rust over time.

It is common to find lines with a larger diameter than the original. To put it simply, the bigger the line, the more you will gain at high rpm, but you will lose at low rpm and vice versa. So, it's up to you but wanting too big won't do much good for everyday use.

To be able to make noise when you want and have the possibility to drive for hours without having a headache, you can install a valve or exhaust flap. The latter is controlled via a button in the living room or a remote control in Bluetooth and allows to divert the gases, directly on the outside, or towards a less silent tube. Thus, you can switch from an exhaust with a silencer to a free exhaust.

It is possible to modify the internals of the engine: Crankshaft, Bearings, Connecting rods, Pistons, Valves, Camshafts... There are more efficient ones in order to increase the power.

However, we are no longer in the small modification, they are not accessible to everyone, it will require equipment and be careful with the parts chosen, with modification of the electronic management of the car if the parameters are not the same as the initial parts.

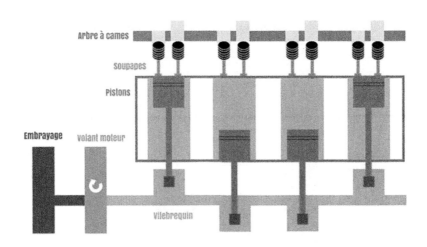

Engine – Cooling

Doing an engine preparation and increasing its power is cool and it makes you happy, we agree!

But often this causes the engine to heat up more.

Most OE cooling systems are oversized and can handle this extra heat and keep the engine running at the right temperature.

It may also be necessary to improve the system, to

Therefore, several solutions exist:

- Decrease the temperature at which the fan is switched on (via the mapping), or by putting a sensor (thermocontact) with a lower temperature)

- Put in a bigger radiator

- Put in a larger or second fan

- Raising the hood: this solution allows for a better evacuation of the hot air circulating under the hood by causing a venturi effect (air suction) at the windshield level and thus a general decrease in temperature.

- Put openings on the hood/air intakes
  Adding additives to the cooling system

- Isolate the exhaust and all heat sources in the engine compartment

Injectors are important components. As their name suggests, they inject fuel into the cylinders.

For large preparations, there are injector modifications with a higher flow rate. However, it is imperative to go through a reprogramming otherwise you run the risk of over-consuming and clogging your engine.

In addition, the installation of large injectors can lead to the need to modify the fuel pump in order to feed them accordingly.

Engine – Flywheel

The flywheel is the link between your clutch and your engine. It is attached to the crankshaft, is part of the clutch, at the engine output before the gearbox.

It is usually made of cast iron and weighs between 5 and 10kg. Therefore it is called flywheel. Due to its mass, it absorbs the jerky energy of the cylinder combustions and releases the energy linearly. It also supports the clutch mechanism because its surface is a support face for the clutch disc.

A toothed wheel is present all around it, which allows starting, and regulation of the engine rotation (TDC sensor).

Lightening the flywheel allows for quicker revs, so power is achieved more quickly and performance is increased. However, it will result in a loss of torque efficiency and a much more erratic engine speed with jerking, as well as an increase in fuel consumption.

On direct injection engines, the oil vapors emitted in the cylinder head are reinjected to be burned by the intake. As a result, they pass through the intake pipes and the valves, where they are deposited to form carbon deposits and therefore fouling.

In order to overcome this phenomenon, which causes engine problems over time and therefore reliability, you can install an oil recuperator.

.

It is placed between your cylinder head cover and the inlet of the vapors. As the vapors pass through it, they condense and settle at the bottom of the collection tray, which you can empty at regular intervals.

Moteur – SWAP

To make a swap consists in exchanging the engine of its car, with another in general more powerful. It is not a small modification.

This can be a less expensive solution than going through multiple modifications that can be time consuming, for a minimal increase in power.

However, it should be noted that any mechanical modification is prohibited by law.

If you persist in your project to change your engine, you should know that you will certainly have to modify the engine mounts, change the cardan shafts, find a suitable gearbox, make a custom wiring harness, reprogram the ECU...

For gasoline engines, several fuels are available. They are differentiated by their octane rating (resistance to auto-ignition, a very harmful phenomenon on gasoline engines - the higher the rating, the less risk), and their components.

- SP95E10: octane number with 9510% ethanol

- SP95: octane number 95

- SP98: octane number 98

- SP98 with additives: octane rating with98 additives to reduce the risk of auto-ignition and engine fouling

- LPG (Liquefied Petroleum Gas): Its composition varies, however, to use it your car must be equipped with a second tank.

- Ethanol E85: octane rating between 100 and 106, it consists of 65 to 85% bioethanol, the rest being SP95. To use it, it will be necessary that it is foreseen in series, or to put in an approved box, or to reprogram the vehicle.

Engine - Fuel

To take advantage of the maximum power of your engine, to reduce the risk of breakdown and to damage it, I can only advise you to run on SP98 with additives.

However, since the year 2000, vehicles are designed to support all the PS.

Give preference to large fuel distributors rather than supermarkets

BODY
AND
INTERIOR

Body and interior – Aesthetics

Many parts exist to modify car bodies, they allow to give character and to personalize.

First, it is possible to modify the color by repainting it, or with a covering, by sticking stickers. You can then make a plain color, or personalized with different patterns and shapes, free rein to your imagination.

It is also possible to add bodywork elements, such as a front blade, bumper or rocker panel addition, fender extensions, a spoiler, air intakes on the sides, on the hood or even on the roof. You can have your windows tinted (beware of the law), change your headlights, put a diffuser...

Otherwise on some models there are complete body kits, which go in place of the original, on which the bumpers are already widened and often more aggressive.

It is important to know that adding aerodynamic parts, such as a spoiler, a diffuser or a flat bottom makes little difference to everyday driving.

It will be necessary to buy performance parts, on specialized sites, often expensive, for them to really bring something. Moreover, the gain will be felt only from a certain speed, that you will not be able to reach legally on the public road.

Modifying the bodywork for a pure performance gain is therefore quite difficult and can be very expensive for a minimal gain.

- However, if you still want to do it, you can buy some pieces like:

- Door panels or a carbon fiber hood can help you reduce the weight (a few kg)

Air intakes on the hood, to improve intake or engine cooling

- Pressure gauges can be installed in conjunction with the engine as performance indicators:

- Water temperature
  Oil temperature and pressure - Turbo pressure
  Exhaust temperature

A multitude of sensors can be installed according to your desires and needs.

It is possible to modify it with more white, blue, or changing colors.

First of all, it is important to know that the lighting is regulated and that a modification can lead to a non- compliance with the technical control.

To change the style, aftermarket headlights exist, and will be quite different from the original.

Otherwise it is possible to simply modify the bulbs and depending on the brand or technology halogen, led, or xenon, the lighting distance, color or beam dispersion will be different.

It is the same for the interior, if your bulbs seem old with a yellowish color, I can only advise you to buy leds. You can find them for about ten euros on the internet.

If you want to put bucket seats, to have more enveloping seats and give a sporty style, nothing forbids you. However, beware of seats that don't have airbags, or you'll have to shunt the beam.

Try to keep as much as possible of the fasteners and original seat rails.

Harnesses are however forbidden on open roads, so you will have to keep the original belt for the technical control.

Be careful when putting racing bucket seats, too radical, they can be very uncomfortable for a production car.

Especially if you make long journeys.

To customize your interior, simply is possible to:

- Change the steering wheel (be careful when dismantling and keep the airbag)

- Change the gear knob

- Put on pallet extensions if you have them

- Modify plastic pedals by using aluminum shims. You can find them ready to install for your model.

- Floor mats are often overlooked, but new or colored mats make your vehicle look clean and new.

- Mounting door sills

- Covering, or repainting certain elements

- Changing your audio system

- Put an armrest

- Change the lighting of the living area and the meter

- Add lights

MODIFICATION AND ELECTONIC BOX

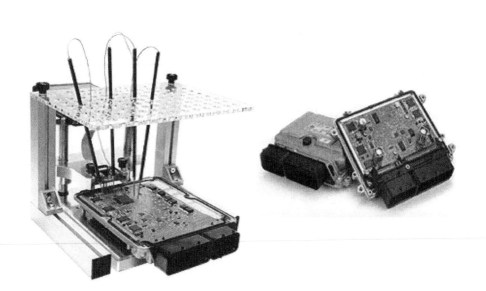

With the arrival of electronics, all manufacturers have adopted the OBD (On Board Diagnostic) standard. This is a diagnostic plug that allows anyone with the right tools to plug in and read or even modify certain parameters.

So, I advise you to buy an ELM327 OBD2. It is a small box that you can find for about ten euros on the internet. It plugs directly into the diagnostic socket, and you will be able to see the values of the sensors of your car, read and erase the defects, on your phone via an application. In case of a problem, you can easily identify it without having to use the manufacturer's case, and therefore save a hundred euros.

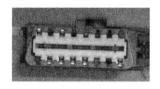

Prise OBD

ELM327

Electronics – Throttle box/PedalBox

These boxes are connected directly to your accelerator pedal. They allow a different driving experience, with the possibility of modifying the response of the pedal. Different modes are selectable to suit your needs or desires.

They give the impression of better recovery and responsiveness, so you'll feel like you're accelerating faster, without changing the torque of engine power.

These boxes are not dangerous, specific to each engine, and most users are very satisfied. If you don't feel like constantly pushing your pedal hard, if you haven't had your car reprogrammed or if your tuner hasn't changed your throttle mapping enough, this box seems to be a good and inexpensive alternative.

It connects to one or more of your car's sensors and is supposed to give you extra power by changing certain parameters (usually the amount of fuel injection).

These boxes contain generic programs, which are not optimized for your vehicle, and even if it can give you a slight power gain it is not the best for your engine.

Moreover, the announced gains are never reached.

If you want to increase the performance, by playing on the electronics and the program of your vehicle, it is better to go through a tuner, who will analyze the state of your car, its mileage, its maintenance and who will develop a program to measure, with tests on bench, and will be able to provide you with figures as well as curves on the gains.

The job of the tuner is to modify your vehicle, it can be performance or design modifications (interior and/or exterior).

For the engine it is often proposed:

Stage 1: Reprogramming of the computer with power increase

Stage 2: Direct 2Intake/Dynamics/Sport Air Filter + Exhaust after catalyst + Dump Valve + Exchanger

Stage 3: Stage 3parts + 2Big turbo + Decatalyser

Stage 4 and + : Stage parts + High flow 3injectors + Reinforced clutch, forge engine internals,

The tuners have their own engine engineers, to guarantee a personalized development, with a gain in performance and engine reliability in all circumstances. They also have their own technicians, to be able to offer you periodic maintenance operations or the installation of performance parts.

Electronics – Reprogramming

Reprogramming aims to increase the engine's performance by increasing its efficiency, and also to reduce fuel consumption.

The electronic control unit (ECU), controls the whole engine. Reprogramming consists of modifying the internal programs of the ECU via a computer, such as fuel injection, ignition, knocking, richness, air flow, etc...

Thus, after tests and measurements on a test bench, the tuner can intervene on several parameters such as: the speed, the turbo pressure, the opening of the injectors, the richness, the intake and exhaust temperatures, etc...

Reprogramming is a profession. Ask around and go to trusted centers, which are known, which will be able to accompany you and provide you with guarantees.

Conclusion

So there are a multitude of operations, modifications and customizations to be made, depending on what you want to achieve and your budget.

Don't do it if you don't feel up to it or if you don't have the tools to do it. Calling in a professional can save you time, trouble and damage to your car.

Conclusion

In order to improve performance, here are the points to focus on in order of importance :

- The pilot

- - The tires

- - The frame

- The engine

Choose modifications according to what you want to achieve and your budget. We will not prepare in the same way a rally type vehicle and another one to do circuit.

In the same way, if you drive 2000 kms/year with a pleasure car and a vehicle used every day, you must adapt the modifications according to the use.

In addition, don't forget that rigorous maintenance is essential to keep your car in good condition. So don't hesitate to perform your maintenance more frequently than recommended by the manufacturer.

Conclusion

I hope this book has helped you understand how it works and what modifications can be made to your car.

There are countless technical solutions and possibilities, so you should do your homework first.

If you have any doubts, do not hesitate to contact a preparer, who will be able to advise you and propose solutions adapted to your needs.

If there are any topics you would like to discuss, feel free to let me know what you would like by sharing a review on the product page of this book.

A constructive advice/opinion will be welcome.

Appendix: Tire Load and Speed Ratings

Indice de charge	Poids en kg	Indice de charge	Poids en kg	Indice de charge	Poids en kg	Indice de charge	Poids en kg
20	80	55	218	79	437	101	825
22	85	58	218	80	450	102	850
24	85	59	243	81	462	103	875
26	90	60	250	82	485	104	900
28	100	61	257	83	487	105	925
30	106	62	265	84	500	106	950
31	109	63	272	85	515	107	975
33	115	64	280	86	530	108	1000
35	121	65	290	87	545	109	1030
37	128	66	300	88	560	110	1060
40	136	67	307	89	580	111	1090
41	145	68	315	90	600	112	1120
42	150	69	325	91	615	113	1150
44	160	70	335	92	630	114	1180
46	170	71	345	93	650	115	1215
47	175	72	355	94	670	116	1250
48	180	73	365	95	690	117	1285
50	190	74	375	96	710	118	1320
51	195	75	387	97	730	119	1360
52	200	76	400	98	750	120	1400
53	206	77	412	99	775		
54	212	78	425	100	800		

Indice	Vitesse maximale	Indice	Vitesse maximale
J	100 km/h	S	180 km/h
K	110 km/h	T	190 km/h
L	120 km/h	U	200 km/h
M	130 km/h	H	210 km/h
N	140 km/h	V	240 km/h
P	150 km/h	W	270 km/h
Q	160 km/h	Y	300 km/h
R	170 km/h	ZR	> 300 km/h

Printed in Great Britain
by Amazon

17706446R00045